WHAT MATTERS
MOST IN SOUTH
SUDAN

Division Destroys, but Unity Builds

STEPHEN MATHIANG

A Note from the Publisher

The publisher wishes to acknowledge and thank Dr Douglas H. Johnson for his invaluable help and support for Africa World Books and its mission of preserving and promoting African cultural and literary traditions and history. Dr Johnson and fellow historians have been instrumental in ensuring that African people remain connected to their past and their identity. Africa World Books is proud to carry on this mission.

© Stephen Mathiang, 2016

ISBN: 978-0-6453010-5-2

All rights reserved.

Cover design, typesetting and layout : Africa World Books

Table of Contents

Dedication

First, I dedicate this book to the Dinka and the Nuer people. Second, I dedicate it to the rest of the South Sudanese people and other peace-loving people of this world.

Acknowledgements

I am thankful to my good editor, Wilson N. Macharia, and also to my creative designer, Mary Maganga, for a job well done.

Above all, I am happy to express my sincere thanks to my dear wife, Elizabeth Agot Leek, and our beloved children, Ajoh, Kuch, Alier, Jogaak and Areu as well as my nephew, Kuch Bech Kuch. God brought you in my life with a purpose to make me think critically, write and live for God and others. May He bless you too so that you can bless others in your lifetime!

Preface

In South Sudan, we are now at the initial stages of nation building, a period that calls for a serious thought, soul-searching and self-sacrifice on the part of our national leaders, particularly, and other South Sudanese in general. Anything that may derail this noble exercise of laying down a solid national foundation requires concerted, collective attention to counter it.

The establishment of a concrete national foundation demands the unity of hearts and minds of all the masses of South Sudan. Among these, the Dinka and the Nuer will need to play a greater role due to the fact that they are the largest ethnic groups in South Sudan. They are to unite and lead purposefully in this crucial work of uniting the South Sudanese peoples in the nation building. This is because if they fail in their role, it will be hard for the important task of national building to proceed, and the set national goals will not be realized. We ought remember that the building of the biblical Tower of Babel came to a standstill and later got destroyed because the efforts of those constructing it were scattered by the confusion of their language.

Now these two key communities seem to be at loggerheads with each other, and their misunderstanding is unfortunately being encouraged by some uncaring, inhumane people, some within and others outside South Sudan. To make matters worse, the differences of these two ethnic communities have had a negative effect on the unity of other communities in the nation as well. As a result, instead of all the South Sudanese peoples focusing their full attention on the laying down of their national foundation, they have ended up getting distracted and bogged down by the so called Dinka-Nuer war. And unless the differences between the Dinka and the Nuer are amicably and urgently resolved and lasting unity between the two communities realized, the vital task of nation building will be hindered, and the future of South Sudan will remain bleak.

There is no way South Sudan will become stable as a nation and move smoothly along the path of development while the Dinka and the Nuer are engaged in a war aimed at the selfish goal of determining who is superior at the local level at the expense of national interests. Considering how costly these ethnic conflicts are, treating them with indifference will be costly both to the two communities and to South Sudan as a nation.

The purpose of this book is to create an early awareness of the magnitude of the problem and mobilize God-fearing and all peace-loving people in and outside South Sudan to seek ways of addressing the simmering issues that threaten the peaceful co-existence of the Dinka and the Nuer. The other objective of writing the book is to seek to restore the unity of the two communities and, ultimately, the unity of the nation.

I wish you read the book and join the peace-building effort in South Sudan! For the Prince of Peace says, "Blessed are the peacemakers, for they will be called sons of God" (Matt.5:9).

Introduction

If the Dinka and the Nuer continue to differ and fight each other, they will destroy themselves now and, over time, the entire nation of South Sudan. But if they peacefully resolve their differences, forgive one another, and unite and live and work together as brothers and sisters, they will build themselves up and have a brighter future. They will also influence other tribes to unite and live and work in harmony as they build their nation, the Republic of South Sudan.

As none of us enjoys disunity and destruction among brothers and sisters, and since no one likes his nation to be divided along tribal lines, to become insecure and to live in constant anarchy, the quest for the unity of the Dinka and the Nuer and other ethnic groups in South Sudan is now more urgent than ever. The future of our people and their nation rests squarely on the unity of the Dinka and the Nuer and that of other tribes.

This book seeks to alert all members of the Dinka and the Nuer and all other South Sudanese and other peace-loving people worldwide of the ugly consequences of the Dinka-Nuer conflict. The book also explores ways and means of resolving their differences and uniting them, with the hope that their unity and peaceful co-existence will lead to the unity of the entire nation of South Sudan.

Chapter One looks into the way in which the Dinka-Nuer conflict can destroy South Sudan. In the same chapter, I discuss at length the early history of the Dinka and the Nuer, their similar backgrounds, their historical relationship, how they relate to other tribes, the heinous plans targeting the Dinka and the Nuer to make them hurt each other, and the repercussions of Dinka-Nuer war to the nation. In Chapter Two, I discuss how the unity of the Dinka and the Nuer can strengthen South Sudan and make it a great nation. This sums up the importance of supporting the unity of the two communities and the perception of the way in which their unity can lead to the unity of the whole country.

I encourage you to read this book with an open mind and with the interest of both Dinka and Nuer and the entire nation at heart. Nobody has a monopoly of knowledge, and this book may not contain all the prerequisites for durable solution to the Dinka-Nuer issue and other national problems. But I believe it contains some of the answers, and reading it will provoke the other answers through other people. Moreover, it is written by one who understands the state of affairs of South Sudan, one who has seen it all so far as fighting for nationhood and declaration of independence are concerned. It is therefore a wakeup call for all those who desire to see the crucial issues that face this nation satisfactorily addressed.

If we own our problems, we can easily address them. But if others solve them for us, we will neither own the solution nor care about it in the end. And before long, we will relapse into the same undesirable condition.

Chapter One

How the Dinka and the Nuer Can Destroy South Sudan

The Genesis of the Dinka and the Nuer

According to Wikipedia, the free encyclopedia, the Nilotes are peoples indigenous to the Nile Valley and speak Nilotic languages, also spoken in South Sudan, Uganda, Kenya and northern Tanzania. Maa, spoken by the Maasai, is one of those languages. The Nilotes include the Luo, the Kalenjin, the Dinka, the Nuer, the Shilluk, the Ateker, and other Maa-speaking peoples, each of which is a cluster of several ethnic groups. In other words, the Maa languages are a group of closely related eastern Nilotic languages spoken in parts of Kenya and Tanzania by more than a million people altogether. They are subdivided into North and South Maa. Ateker or ŋaTekerin is a common name for the closely related Jie, Karamojong, Turkana, Toposa, Nyangatom and Teso. The Maa languages are related to the Lotuko languages spoken in South Sudan.

The Nilotes form the majority of the population in South Sudan. They also constitute the second largest group of peoples inhabiting the African Great Lakes Region (after the Bantu peoples), with a notable presence in south-western Ethiopia as well. The Nilotes mainly adhere to Christianity and traditional faiths, commonly known as African Traditional Religion (ATR).

The Luo (also spelled Lwo) are several ethnically and linguistically related Nilotic people groups in Africa that inhabit an area stretching from South Sudan and Ethiopia, through northern Uganda and eastern Congo (DRC), into western Kenya, and the Mara region of Tanzania. Their Luo-related languages belong to the Nilotic group and thus form part of the larger eastern Sudanic family. In most classifications, the eastern Sudanic languages are a group of nine families of languages that may constitute a branch of the Nilo-Saharan language family. Eastern Sudanic languages are spoken from southern Egypt to northern Tanzania.

Within the Nilotic languages, the Luo

together with the Dinka and Nuer form the western Nilotic branch. Groups within the Luo nation include the Shilluk, the Anuak, the Acholi, the Alur, the Padhola, the Joluo (Kenyan and Tanzanian Luo), the Boor, and the Luwo. The Belanda Boor (or Boor) is an ethnic group numbering 40,000 to 50,000 people living in the South Sudanese states of Western Equatoria and Western Bahr el Ghazal. They speak the Belanda Boor language. However, most of them are bilingual in Belanda Viri.

The Luwo (also called *Jur Chol,* and *luo Jur*) are an ethnic group in the western parts of South Sudan in Jur River County and Wau County of Western Bahr el Ghazal State and in Aweil Center County of Northern Bahr el Ghazal State. They are part of a larger group of peoples ethno-linguistically related to the Luo peoples of East Africa. They are considered part of the larger ethnic cluster known as the Nilotes.

The Joluo and their language, Dholuo, are also known as the "Luo proper", eponymous name of the larger group. The historical separation between these groups is estimated at about eight centuries. Dispersion from the Nilotic homeland in South Sudan was, presumably, triggered by the turmoil of the

Muslim conquest of Sudan. The individual groups over the last few centuries can, to some extent, be traced to the respective group's oral history.

The Dinka people are an ethnic group inhabiting the Bahr el Ghazal region of the Nile basin, Jonglei and parts of southern Kordufan and Upper Nile regions. The Dinkas are mainly agri-pastoral people, relying on cattle herding at riverside camps in the dry season and growing millet (*awuou*) and other varieties of grains (*rap*) in fixed settlements during the rainy season. They number around 4.5 million people, according to the 2008 Sudan census, and constitute about 18% of the population of the entire country. They constitute the largest ethnic tribe in South Sudan. The Dinka, or *Muonyjang* (singular) and *Jeng* (plural), as they refer to themselves, is one of the branches of the River Lake Nilotes. They are mainly agri-pastoral people of the Nile Valley and the African Great Lakes region who speak Nilotic languages, including the Nuer and Luo.

The Dinkas are sometimes noted for their height. Together with the Tutsi of Rwanda, they are believed to be the tallest people in Africa. Roberts and Bainbridge reported the average

height of 182.6 cm (5 ft. 11.9 in) in a sample of
52 Dinka Ager and 181.3 cm (5 ft. 11.4 in) in
227 Dinka Ruwengs measured in 1953–1954.
However, it seems that today's male Dinka is
shorter, possibly as a consequence of under-
nutrition and other negative effects arising
from conflicts. An anthropometric survey of
the Dinka men and war refugees in Ethiopia,
published in 1995, found a mean height of 176.4
cm (5 ft. 9.4 in). Other studies of comparative
historical height data and nutrition place the
Dinka as the tallest people in the world.

The Dinka people have no centralized
political authority. They comprise many
independent but interlinked clans. Certain of
those clans traditionally provide ritual chiefs,
known as the "masters of the fishing spear" or
beny de bith. These provide leadership to the
entire community, and their position appears
to be hereditary in part. Yet they also have
elected chiefs to oversee and preside over their
local affairs. Today, most Dinkas have embraced
Christianity. The rest belong to the ATR. Islam
claims only a small percentage of the entire
population.

Their language, called Dinka or "thu⊠ŋjäŋ"
(*tho⊠ de muonyja⊠*), is one of the Nilotic

languages of the eastern Sudanic language family. In the Dinka language, the name Dinka means "People". It is written using the Latin alphabet with a few additions.

The Nuer people, on the other hand, are a Nilotic ethnic group mainly found the Nile Valley. They are concentrated in South Sudan, with some representatives also found in south-western Ethiopia. They speak the Nuer language, which is a part of the Nile-Saharan language family.

The Nuer language is a Nilo-Saharan language of the Western Nilotic group. It is spoken by the Nuer people of South Sudan and by people in western Ethiopia (Gambela region). Nuer language has a Latin-based alphabet. There are also several dialects of Nuer, though all are written in the same way. For example, a 'k' pronounced in the Jikany dialect is dropped in other dialects despite appearing in the Nuer orthography. Nuer is one of eastern and central Africa's most widely spoken languages. The language is called *thoknaath,* meaning the tongue of the people.

There are different dialects spoken by the Nuer groups that live in different parts of South Sudan. Those in Ethiopia include Gajaak and

Gajiok. In Gajaak there is Chie Chaany, Chie Reang, Chie Waw, Chie Nyinjani and Thiang. The Nuer of the Nasir region are called Gajiok, and those in Waat are called Lou. There are also Gaweer and Jikueichieng.

Historically, cattle have had the highest symbolic, religious and economic value among the Nuer. Cattle are particularly important in their role of paying the bride price, whereby they are given by a husband's family to the wife's family. Like the Dinka, the Nuers are an agri-pastoral people.

The Nuer (Nuäär) believe that God is the spirit of the sky or the spirit who is in the sky. He is referred to as *Kuoth Nhial* (God in Heaven), the Creator. But the Nuer also regard the rain, lightning and thunder as the coming of God, and that the rainbow is the necklace of God. They also regard the sun, the moon and a couple of other material entities as manifestations or signs of God, who after all is a spirit. The spirits of the air above are believed to be the most powerful of the lesser spirits. There are also spirits associated with clan-spear names. One of them is Wiw, which is a spirit of war, associated with thunder.

The Nuers believe that when a person dies,

the flesh, the life and the soul go separate ways. The flesh is committed to the earth, while the breath or life goes back to God (Kuoth). They say that the soul, that represents the human individuality and personality, remains alive as a shadow or a reflection, and it departs together with the ox that is sacrificed at the place of the ghosts. Today, majority of the Nuer are Christians. The rest belong to the African Traditional Religion. A very, very small percentage of the population has embraced Islam.

Similarity between the Dinka and the Nuer

The Dinka and the Nuer are pastoralists, though both tribes also do some farming, but on a small scale. According to recent statistics from the Ministry of Agriculture, Forestry, Tourism, Animal Resources and Fisheries, South Sudan has an estimated 11.7 million cattle, 12.4 million goats and 12.1 million sheep. Most of these domestic animals are owned by the Dinka and the Nuer. These communities keep their animals mainly for milk, for bride price, for meat and to sell for their financial needs. One's wealth is measured by the number of cattle they own. Their cattle are not confined for zero grazing; they are allowed to wander from one place to another in search of water and pasture. Cattle are their primary source of livelihood and a mark of cultural prestige.

Another source of livelihood for the Dinka and the Nuer is farming. This is mainly subsistence form of farming. Every household has a small garden around or near its base. The cereals that are mainly grown include sorghum, maize and millet. Other crops include beans, sesame, pumpkins and groundnuts. Were they to consider large-scale farming, there is a huge local and international market awaiting their products.

The Dinka and the Nuer depend on fish from the Nile and its tributaries. They supply the local markets with dried and fresh fish. They also hunt wild animals for meat. On a limited scale, these Nilotes benefit from different varieties of seasonal wild fruits.

Judging by physical features, an outsider would find it difficult to distinguish between a Dinka and a Nuer. This is because both are generally tall, dark and smooth-skinned. These peoples share some cultural characteristics, like the removal of six lower teeth before or after one attains the adolescent age of 14. In some cases, the Dinka and the Nuer, particularly men, have facial scars on the forehead that are made with a sharp knife. And since this ritual is done outside the medical facility—and hence done without anesthesia—you can imagine how painful it is! When it is being performed on men, they are supposed to demonstrate courage by not shedding a tear while the operation is going on; if they cry, they earn themselves the loathed title of coward. But those who endure the excruciating pain valiantly are regarded as 'real men'.

I gather that during the time of colonialism in Sudan, there was an arrogant Briton, a District Commissioner based in a certain town in Bahr el Ghazal. In the course of his administration, he accused the local chiefs of being defiant. One day, he ordered all the chiefs to come to his office, and he asked them, "Why do you not carry out orders promptly? Is there any medicine that you take to make you that arrogant? I would be more than glad to take it also so as to behave in the same manner."

The poor chiefs told him that they did not have such a medicine and that they dealt with him in their right senses. But the white man was not satisfied and ordered them to return to their homes and bring him 'the medicine' the following day, failure to which he would have them all arrested. This order from their imperial boss made them feel very confuse, and they departed his office forlorn, wondering how they were going to satisfy this impossible demand so as to escape jail. They were more than aware that their foreign boss was a hard taskmaster who never budged on issues, and the following day they were to meet him and produce what never existed. They were in a real tight spot and hence, very sad. Their people too were convinced that the white man was making unrealistic demand to get a way of picking a quarrel with them and get an opportunity to harm them.

In the course of this confusion, an old man came forward and rebuked them for not knowing the medicine they were supposed to give the white man. He then told these chiefs to eat and take life easy because he was going to get them out of the dilemma. To this, skeptics booed and told him to stop joking with such a grave matter that put their lives on the line. They even asked him to show them the medicine or "just keep quiet". The old man said he would not show it to them, but offered to appear before the colonialist with them the following day, carrying the mysterious medicine with him. Then he would show it to the DC in their presence. Otherwise, he would just leave them to tackle their problem if they were to refuse his advice. Desperate for a solution to their problem, the chiefs reluctantly acceded and prepared to meet their white boss with this old man the following day.

On the following day, the old man trekked with the nervous chiefs to the white man's office, and when they got there, they sat down on the rough ground in front of their unkind boss. When the District Commissioner saw this odd, old man sitting behind the chiefs with his small, closed basket, he asked bewilderedly, "Who is this man, and why is he in your company?" In reply, the chiefs told their boss that he carried the medicine that he had asked for.

Excited and apprehensive at the same time, the imperialist called upon the old man to come forward and display his mysterious concoction and, better still, demonstrate how it is used. It was a great opportunity for the white man to finally see the secret behind the 'arrogance' of the Dinka male. Ironically, even the chiefs were themselves eager to see what made them behave the way they behaved in the hope of getting a deeper understanding of themselves.

At this point, the old man walked proudly to where the commissioner sat, all eyes on him, and when asked by the white man whether he had this medicine that made people "brave and stubborn", he confidently replied, "Yes". He made a step close to the white man and added, "Let me show it to you and how it is used". With everyone keenly following what was going on, the old man put his hand into his basket and drew out its contents: a small fishing spear and a small sharp knife. The District Commissioner said he knew what these crude instruments were used for but insisted that what he wanted was medicine. Even his countrymen wondered why the old man termed them as the medicine. But the old man insisted that these instruments constituted the 'medicine' the white man was after.

To end the stalemate and hopefully get an opportunity to punish the old man, the adamant Briton ordered the old man to prove how these traditional instruments were used as medicine "for arrogance and stubbornness". At this point, the bold old man took charge and explained that the spear was used to remove the lower teeth, while the knife was used to make the facial marks, including the long running lines across the forehead. He went ahead and said that for one to be a real, brave, stubborn man like a Dinka, he had to manfully endure these painful marks of cultural initiation.

As this old man went on with his explanation, the British administrator took good counsel but became somewhat nervous as what made up the actual manhood of Dinka became quite clear. Maybe, one of the questions that came to his mind was: *If these people do not fear the excruciating pain that goes with their skin being cut with these unsterilized metallic objects, how will they docilely follow my orders as I seek to impose my will on them?* He kept wondering within himself. As the British administrator nodded in response to the wisdom behind the old man's allegorical explanations, the chiefs completely agreed at last with the old man's viewpoint.

Finally, the old man offered the nervous colonialist the opportunity to become brave like a Dinka man by going through the initiation— without crying. And before he answered, the old man asked the chiefs to help in holding down their boss to receive the painful signs of the actual manhood. But as the chiefs stood to help the old man to apply the 'medicine' on this Briton, he fled, leaving the chiefs and the rest of the people laughing and praising the old man for his unique wisdom. Although the white man remained their boss, he began to treat these people with respect. This story reminds us of the following Wiseman's words:

I also saw under the sun this example of wisdom that greatly impressed me. There was once a small city with only a few people in it. And a powerful king came against it, surrounded it and built huge siege works against it. Now there lived in that city a poor man but wise, and he saved the city by his wisdom. But nobody remembered that poor man. So I said, 'wisdom is better than strength.' But the poor man's wisdom is despised, and his words are no longer heeded (Eccl.9:13-16).

Just like the poor man of the book of Ecclesiastes, the poor old Dinka man might have at first been despised by the chiefs, but they eventually saw the wisdom of his words. His wisdom saved the chiefs and his entire community, boosted their heroic fame, and made the white boss naïve and friendly to them in the end. The Dinka and the Nuer attribute their manhood partly to these painful rituals. But such cultural practices are dying away slowly, especially among urban dwellers.

In terms of language similarity, the Dinka and the Nuer share many words in common, though the dialects differ slightly. During the time of my early education, I used to joke with my Nuer colleagues by challenging them to give the Nuer equivalent of words in Dinka, which invariably turned out to be Dinka words spoken with a dialect. To this I would jokily reply: "The Nuer have no language of their own; they speak Dinka". Then my colleagues would reply, "It is the Dinka who have no language of their own and therefore, find themselves speaking Nuer." And all of us would laugh, indirectly agreeing that the Dinka and the Nuer are brothers, a people with common ancestry.

The Dinka and the Nuer often intermarry. Thus, there are uncles, cousins, nephews, aunts, fathers and mothers who somehow act as a bridge for the two communities.

The Dinka and the Nuer are proud and courageous people who sometimes stubbornly refuse to forgive and forget any wrong done to them, whether by outsiders or even by their own people. Some of them can be very provocative and aggressive as they deal with one another and with the outsiders. They have a sort of domineering spirit which makes others level them as being oppressive and leadership-hunger-thirsting people. They attach unique value to being thought of as warriors. The Dinka and the Nuer do not fear any threat, be it the threat of death. But as we know the current world does not reward pride, arrogance, unforgiving spirit, provocation, aggressiveness, domineering, oppressiveness and defiance. Yet seeing from a broad, global perspective, these supposed traits are not unique to the Dinka and the Nuer alone, for other ethnicities in and outside South Sudan are obsessed with them.

Historical Relationship between the Dinka and the Nuer

As people who share the same ancestry, I believe the Dinka and the Nuer might have coexisted harmoniously sometime in the past. This is evidenced by the way the two communities have been living side by side in South Sudan. Even if they were sometimes involved in territorial disputes, these were minor conflicts that are common with any given society under the sun. These are the kind of disputes that can occur at the family, community, national, regional or global level.

The relationship of the various ethnic groups in southern Sudan was greatly affected in 19th century by the invasion of the Ottomans, the Arabs and, eventually, the British. Some ethnic groups made peace with the imperial attackers, while others did not. This, in effect, pitted ethnic groups against each other during the time that the nation was ruled by foreigners. For example, some sections of the Dinka were more accommodative of the British rule than were the Nuer. As a result, these Dinkas treated the Nuers as hostile because of this resistance. This is to say that the hostility that developed between these two ethnic groups ironically had the British rule as its origin.

Unfortunately, after Sudan gained her independence from Britain on 1 January 1956, some bitterness continued to simmer between the Dinka and the Nuer. As a result, minor disputes along certain Dinka-Nuer borders kept breaking but were addressed by the locals or with the help of the government.

The major significant dispute happened

between the two communities as a result of political disagreement between some Dinka and Nuer politicians and military commanders during the war of liberation in 1983-2005. This occurred during the formation of the Sudan People's Liberation Movement (SPLM) and Sudan People's Liberation Army (SPLA) in Bilpam, Ethiopia in 1983. The resulting conflict caused huge loss of human life and property, displacement of some local communities on both sides and even delayed the common goal of attaining independence because a lot of effort was dissipated in fighting each other instead of fighting their common enemy.

For instance, for reasons best known to him, Dr. Riek Machar decided to topple Dr. John Garang from the SPLM/SPLA leadership in August 1991. As this movement did not represent Dinka's or Nuer's interests alone—though the two rival leaders were from these two ethnic communities—Riek's coup was logically seen by many in and outside Sudan as an independent problem within the SPLM/SPLA. The problem that led to Riek's coup was not specifically caused by or related to the Dinka and Nuer communities. Instead, it was an issue within the South Sudanese liberation movement, affecting all the concerned tribes in the whole Sudan. And if Riek was to succeed in his coup attempt, the whole movement was to fall behind him to continue along.

But to show the magnitude of the poor relationship that existed between the Dinka and the Nuer, and also to show the naivety of the two communities, this coup failed and lost its focus and ended up pitting the Nuer against the Dinka, with a great loss of lives and property on both sides. Yet what had caused all this is the fact that Riek happened to be a Nuer, while Garang was a Dinka; hence, the poor guys ended up fighting each other for the defense of their own tribesmen instead of pursuing the national cause for which the SPLM/SPLA had been conceived.

In 2006, the Nuer was one of the tribes that resisted disarmament most strongly. Members of the Nuer White Army, a group of armed youths that is autonomous in view of the fact it acts independently of the tribal elders' authority, refused to lay down its weapons. It is not until mid-2006 that the White Army was finally subdued. The organization that succeeded it and took the same name was formed in 2011 to fight other armed groups, especially in Jonglei

State. Although White Army had not been formed with the express intention of fighting the Dinka, minor skirmishes continued to occur along the Dinka-Nuer borders.

Seemingly as a reverberation of those pre-independence conflicts, there have been political wrangles simmering within the SPLM ruling party since the birth of South Sudan on 9 July 2011, pitting the former Vice President Dr. Riek Machar against President Salva Kiir Mayardit. And the alleged cause of this was that the former was intent on assuming authority in this party, with the desire of seeking the highest political office in the land on the party ticket during a general election that was supposed to take place in 2015. But the election was preempted by the political feuds that culminated in the war that erupted in Juba on 16 December 2015.

Under normal circumstances, this unhealthy political game should have been seen in the eyes of national politics and interpreted as normal resistance against the government of the day and suppressed with the usual machinery. But because of the unhealthy relationship between the Dinka and the Nuer, and due to the fact that the President is a Dinka and Dr. Riek is a

Nuer, the fight took an ugly, ethnic dimension, pitting the Dinka against the Nuer.

This war that started in Juba, the centre of political misunderstanding, quickly spread to the countryside, especially to the Dinka and the Nuer areas, causing huge loss of human lives, unnecessary displacements of local population and destruction of property. In the same way as Riek's coup of 1991, the political eruption in Juba in 2015 lost its focus and pitted the Dinka against the Nuer instead.

Although politicians from both sides have a healthy attitude towards politics, enjoying life and even buying each other tea in hotels in urban centres, the Dinka and the Nuer villagers regard each other as enemies, perpetuating the war by going after each other's throat. Juba government terms the war as a conflict between government soldiers and the rebels, but others see it as a tribal war between the Dinka and the Nuer. But irrespective of how it is viewed, the fact of the matter is that the government and the rebels are not in good terms now, and neither are the Dinkas and the Nuers. And unless the two warring parties and the rest of the people of South Sudan, including the government, take urgent action to address this pointless dispute, things will move from bad to worse.

How the Dinka and Nuer Relate with Other Tribes

The relationship between the Dinka and the Nuer and their neighbouring tribes in South Sudan has never been cordial. As pointed out earlier in this book, the Dinka and the Nuer are agri-pastoralists. They move around with their animals in search of pasture and water, especially during dry seasons. Needless to say, their nomadic life usually exposes them to conflict with other nomadic communities. The causes of such conflict include competition over grazing land and water as well as cattle rustling.

Also, since pastoralists (herders who do not practise zero grazing but allow cattle to wander from place to place) are constantly having disputes with farmers, the Dinka and the Nuer are ever in conflict with their neighbouring farming communities. At the time of writing this book, the Dinka and the Mundari are pitted against some farming tribes in western and central Equatoria states.

Examples of such disputes are common between the Dinka and the Murle, the Dinka and the Mundari, the Dinka and the Shilluk, the Nuer and the Murle, the Nuer and the Anyuak, the Nuer and the Shilluk, among others. Nor is the fallout of such disputes confined to rural areas; their negative effects are evident in the relationship between urban dwellers as well. The result has been a poisoned political atmosphere at the local and national level that is brought about by the animosity emanating from the ethnic disputes. Needless to say, people will naturally take sides in national politics, and there is no way they will agree with those whom they perceive as causing problems to their people at the grassroots level.

The constantly simmering problem between the Dinka and the Nuer sometimes drags other tribes into the conflict as well. As result, these smaller communities begin to view the two big tribes as troublemakers and, as a result, they develop hatred for them. For instance, when the Dinka and the Nuer turned against each other during the twenty-first year war of independence, the resulting suffering affected other tribes as well, with huge loss of human lives and property. The local strife even prolonged the national struggle. Again, the Juba conflict of 2013, which some people termed as a tribal war between the Dinka and the Nuer, affected other people of South Sudan. Lives and property were lost, not to mention displacement both in some urban and rural areas.

In certain towns, the Dinkas and the Nuers are accused of not respecting other people's property. This brings about the existence of poor relationship between them and people from other communities. People of these communities sometimes find it easier to deal with foreigners than with their countrymen from the Dinka and the Nuer tribes. It is common knowledge that people from Equatoria region, for example, prefer to rent or lease their properties to foreigners like Somalis, Ethiopians, Eritreans, Sudanese or Egyptians instead of giving them out to fellow countrymen from the Dinka and the Nuer communities. This shows the level of the poor relationship that exists between them and the Dinka and the Nuer.

Some of the peace-loving South Sudanese communities view the Dinka and the Nuer as violent and domineering and, as a result, fear to relate with them. Very often when they do it, it is out of fear or intimidation.

Another factor that is behind the poor relationship between the Dinka and the Nuer and other ethnic communities in South Sudan is their huge numbers that make them dominate national politics, businesses, the armed forces, and other sectors of the economy. This ubiquity and seeming monopoly has made people from other communities resent them. Nor are people from these two communities more visible than others only when they are benefiting materially; they are more visible in death as well. During the last two bloody civil wars in Sudan, the percentage of the Dinkas and the Nuers who died to total deaths in the nation was very high in comparison with that of the other tribes. So when it comes to national defence and the dangers thereof, other tribes appreciate the fact that there are many Dinkas and Nuer in the military.

For example, I am told that during the long bloody civil war in Sudan, some of the other tribes in encouraged their young people to pursue their education and business in and outside Sudan with the hope that the Dinka and the Nuer plus a few other people were going to fight and liberate the nation. And they did, and those who pursued their education are now enjoying the results of the suffering of their brothers and sisters in South Sudan.

When it comes to sharing the national cake, the Dinkas and the Nuers feel that it is only logical that they should have the lion's share due to their big numbers. But this does not go down well with the small tribes, for they feel that fair distribution of resources is not done. Another reason the Dinka and the Nuer remain convinced is that it is their right to have the bigger share is because of their role in the war for nationhood and protecting their country from internal and external aggression.

The criteria to use in sharing out the national cake is, however, a very complicated issue that calls for a broad, logical thinking among South Sudanese people. But in my opinion, the Dinka and the Nuer should allow their brothers and sisters to give them their share of the cake instead of demanding it, whether verbally or through other means. Of course the rule of the thumb anywhere is that few fight the war, but all must appear at the meal table. The supposed unfair distribution of the national cake among the sons and daughters of the land is part of the reason why people talk of the Dinka-Nuer domination, making other communities resent them.

But for the sake of unity and peaceful co-existence between the Dinka and the Nuer, for the sake of unity and peaceful co-existence between these big communities and their neighbours, and for the sake of the unity of the nation as a whole, there is urgent need to promote cohesion among all the communities of South Sudan, beginning with the cohesion of the Dinka and the Nuer. To do so, however, calls for rare tact and objectivity that is informed by good background knowledge of the communities' past, not just dealing with the symptoms but searching deeper for the underlying causes of the current problems.

Inappropriate Plans against the Dinkas and the Nuer

As the Dinkas and the Nuers are blessed with numbers, constituting a great percentage of the South Sudanese population and being thus perceived by other local communities as a threat, some unkind politicians from smaller tribes have conceived of all manner of ways of reducing the size of their population and making them to be like other smaller tribes, if not fewer. One such method is that of fanning animosity between the Dinka and the Nuer so as to make them to fight and scale down the numbers of each other. Moreover, they do this with the awareness that these two communities are good fighters and have weaknesses that make them susceptible to duping by people with malicious intentions into turning against each another. That way when the Dinka and the Nuer get mad at each other, these evil plotters feel good and laugh sarcastically, prodding them to continue with the 'ethnic cleansing'. They neither care for the wellbeing of the two communities nor for the general welfare of the people of South Sudan.

But there are also external enemies of the South Sudanese and their nation as well. These know very well that they can't achieve their goal if the Dinka and the Nuer are solidly united, for they can be ready to valiantly protect any national 'needle' from being taken by an outsider. Such foreign enemies are aware that the only way to realize their evil goal is to trick the narrow-minded, selfish South Sudanese politicians to make their fellow tribesmen (the Dinka and the Nuer) to use their might and strong will to kill each other. That is what has been happening during the twenty-one-year Sudan civil war: the two communities were turned against each other, resulting in unnecessary death toll and wanton destruction of property and internal displacements of poor people from both sides. And today, both the local traitors and external vampires are shedding crocodile tears at the tombs of the poor Dinka and Nuer people whose perishing they actually facilitated. Although they are very vocal about the appalling conditions of the displaced people who have become refugees within and outside their country, these greedy people revel in seeing the Dinka and Nuer homelands left to wild animals and birds because the people are no more. Better still, they would want the civil war to shift from national dimension to tribal dimension and continue unabated as the Dinka-Nuer war of self-annihilation.

Yet this unfortunate trick that is being played on the Dinka and the Nuer is not new in our continent. A story is told of how the rabbit taunted the elephant, telling him, "That big body of yours won't help you in a rope contest with me." Feeling slighted, the elephant challenged the rabbit to choose a day when he would prove the rabbit wrong. The rabbit then went to the rhino and taunted him in the same way he had the elephant, provoking the rhino to agree to a contest on the same day the rabbit was supposed to tug with the elephant.

The rabbit had decided that the contest takes place on a mountain, with him on one side and his opponent on the other. On the day of the contest, he gave the elephant one side of the rope and, pretending to be going to the other side of the mountain to pull from there, went and gave the rhino the other side of the rope. Then, unknown to either of the actual contestants, the rabbit hid in a nearby bush and started shouting, "Pull....pull!"

At the end of the day, the animals were not only physically drained, but the horn of the rhino was almost coming out and the elephant's tusks dangling uselessly. Meanwhile, the rabbit was on his way home, laughing.

How often this same trick is played on communities in the same nation by outsiders who set them up against each other with the hidden motive of destroying their nation! It is high time the Dinka and the Nuer paused to find out who is making them to get into the useless contest of 'rope pulling' and stop before they get wiped out or have their energy drained in useless work instead of being used in developing themselves and their nation.

Repercussion of the Dinka and the Nuer War

When two elephants fight, they suffer and may even kill each other in the process. Also in the course of their fight, the grass beneath suffers greatly. The small trees nearby suffer, too. Even the bare ground upon which the elephants fight is trampled on with their rough, strong feet. The only parties that enjoy seeing elephants fight and, better still, kill each other are the birds of prey and lions and hyenas. To them, that is food in preparation, which they then eat and move away, leaving the dry bones behind.

But if the elephants knew the dreadful consequences of their fight—their own death, destruction of the grass they feed on, and becoming the food of vultures and other wild beasts—they would think twice before engaging in fighting each other. If someone cheats you all the times, your sanity may require psychiatric test!

Definitely, the Dinka and the Nuer politicians who enjoy seeing their people locked in the deadly elephant-rhino contest have neither the interest of their communities nor those of their nation at heart. What benefit would accrue to them when the Dinka and the Nuer butcher and annihilate themselves? If all they seek is winning a war to create a name for their communities, then they need to reread the above story of the elephant and the rhino to see how much it cost the contestants. They must also remember that pride comes before the fall. What I know for sure is that the Dinka will never wipe out the Nuer or the Nuer the Dinka. And even if one of these esteemed communities were to totally annihilate the other, who would provide the disgraced award to the winner? Perhaps Satan, whom the Bible says comes to kill, to steal and to destroy, would be having the diabolical award to present to the disgraced winner.

What is even sad is that the Dinka-Nuer problem could degenerate into a national problem because there is no way South Sudan can be at peace when two of its communities are at war. This is why the Dinka and Nuer people who used their expertise in instigating the conflict between the Dinka and the Nuer should abandon their devilish scheme, move quickly at this time and use their expertise to bring peace between the two communities for the sake of the nation at large. These communities need each other to live and to protect their nation from any external force.

It is high time that those South Sudanese 'rabbits' who love to see the elephant and rhino destroy each other realized that the destruction of the Dinka and the Nuer is also the destruction of South Sudan as a nation. There is no way South Sudanese can achieve cohesion and gain respect in the community of nations in the absence of the Dinka and the Nuer. The presence of your big, strong brother in the house means security in the house and respect from the neighbours. Even if he sometimes misbehaves in the house, you should see how to make him change instead of wishing him to be out of the scene.

One time in certain village in Dinka land, there were five sons of the same father and mother. Two sons were well built and fearless. In terms of temperament, they were extroverts, their behaviour revealing choleric temperament. The other sons exhibited a mixture of sanguine, phlegmatic and melancholic temperament. To a certain extent, some of them exhibited the character of introverts.

Their forefathers had a fertile, huge piece of land where they kept their many domestic animals. The land fronted a big river which provided continuous supply of fresh water, both for human and animal consumption. Neighbours envied their riches, but they were afraid to invade and take away the possessions of the family due to the presence of its strong sons.

The two strong and brave sons were particularly feared by the fellow villagers, making the neighbours nervous.

Sometimes the strong brothers got mad at their weaker brothers when the latter irritated the former by their actions and words. Whenever these two strong sons fought, they did it ruthlessly and no one dared to separate them peradventure they turn their wrath on him. In their duels, they seemed poised to destroy each other. But they had a unique way of resolving their differences and would eventually reconcile and start living harmoniously again.

Because of their constant quarreling between themselves as well as with their envious neighbours, the five brothers didn't make good use of their prime ancestral land. Their animals were even being stolen by their cunning neighbours. Two of the three brothers got frustrated by their warring brothers' behaviour and tried to destroy them. But the neighbours also had a plan—to destroy the family, beginning with the first two strong brothers and later enslaving or killing the rest and taking possession of their land.

At some point, two of the three weak brothers colluded with some of their neighbours against their two strong brothers. The two naïve brothers lured their strong brothers to get at each other's neck. In the course of the fight, one of them fell down dead. Then the government of the land came, arrested and sentenced the murderer to death. And he had to be hung, since the two sons who encouraged them to fight happily consented to the decision of the court. Then the conspirators, the two brothers and the unkind neighbours, shed crocodile tears over their death. Then the three brothers decided to forget about their dead brothers and continue with life.

But before long, the unkind neighbours planned a concerted effort, killed the two brothers and enslaved the peaceful one. They then plundered the wealth and shared out the land among themselves. Thus, who gained in the end? The neighbours of course!

It is better for a brother to slap you in the face than for an enemy to shower you with flattering words. A bad brother may terribly annoy and tempt you to get rid of him in some way, but for the sake of the continuation and unity of the family, it is always wise to forgive your brother and see how to make peace while both of you are alive. Forgiving your brother is supported even in the Bible, and is worth emulating. We are aware that we too sin against God all the time and require His forgiveness. None of us can claim never to have hurt a brother in their life; therefore, it is imperative for us to forgive each other always. We ought to read Matt. 18:21-35 reflectively to see why we should henceforth embrace forgiveness of each other:

> *Then Peter came to Jesus and asked, 'Lord, how many times shall I forgive my brother when he sins against me? 'Up to seven times?'*
>
> *Jesus answered, 'I tell you, not seven times, but seventy-seven times.*
>
> *Therefore, the kingdom of heaven is like a king who wanted to settle accounts with his servants. As he began the settlement, a man who owned him ten thousand talents was brought to him. Since he was not able to pay, the master ordered that he and his wife and his children and all that he had be sold to repay the debt.*
>
> *The servant fell on his knees before him. 'Be patient with me,' he begged, 'and I will pay back everything.' The servant's master took pity on him, canceled the debt and let him go.*

But when that servant went out, he found one of his fellow servants who owned him a hundred denarii. He grabbed him and began to choke him. 'Pay back what you own me!' he demanded.

His fellow servant fell to his knees and begged him, 'Be patient with me, and I will pay you back.' But he refused. Instead, he went off and had the man thrown into prison until he could pay the debt. When the other servants saw what had happened, they were greatly distressed and went and told their master everything that had happened.

Then the master called the servant in. 'You wicked servant,' he said, 'I canceled all that debt of yours because you begged me to. Shouldn't you have had mercy on your fellow servant just as I had on you?'

In anger his master turned him over to the jailers to be tortured, until he should pay back all he owed.

'This is how my heavenly Father will treat each of you unless you forgive your brother from your heart.'

As man is born into ancient mistakes, live in mistakes, make his own mistakes, and live his and others' mistakes behind for the next generation to inherit, he has an inescapable obligation to forgive others' mistakes done to him as he expects others to forgive his mistakes done unto them.

Concerning the external 'rabbits' who are intent on seeing South Sudan 'elephants' and 'rhino' rope-pulling contest continues, they neither love to see the 'elephant' and 'rhino' live in peace and progress. Nor do they like seeing other people of the new nation living peacefully within their nation's borders. And they won't be satisfied until they see South Sudanese people get mad at each other; they won't be satisfied until the South Sudanese take their lives into their own hands and leave their natural wealth for the external 'rabbits' to greedily loot and plunder it.

But what the external 'rabbits' should know is that if you dig and cover a deep hole for someone to fall into, you may fall into the same hole yourself. For the wise man says, "If a man digs a pit, he will fall into it; if a man rolls a stone, it will roll back on him" (Prov.26:27). See also in the book of Esther how Haman ended up dangling on the seventy-five-feet gallows that he had deviously planned for his arch-enemy Mordecai. This is not to mention the account in the book of Daniel that tells how he escaped the jaws of hungry lions which later crushed to pieces the bones of his enemies.

There was once an old man in our village called Herjok Kur. This man had sons and daughters, and his sons grew and became very powerful. The sons were living peacefully with each other as well as with other people. One day, he called them and told them, saying:

My sons, people are not good. If they see you loving one another and living in peace, they will not be happy. Instead, they will start looking for ways of dividing and turning you against each other. To do that, a cunning neighbour will pretend to befriend you, but as time goes, he will approach every one of you privately and say, 'Your brother so and so isn't happy with you and has been talking ill about you.' After spreading hatred among you to make you get mad at each other, he then withdraws from visiting and interacting with you. With your minds and hearts thus poisoned, you henceforth begin to relate with each other suspiciously. You stop regarding each other as brothers but as enemies. As a result, one day when you come together to address some family issues and each of you desire to air his viewpoint, you immediately recall the words of your cunning friend and begin to feel angry with each other for no reason. As a result, fighting among you will ensue. Then the innocent neighbours who know of your past harmonious relationship will shout and rush to separate you, saying, 'The children of so and so are fighting each other; let's rush and rescue them from killing each other.' After hearing that, the man who causes the problem among you will materialize and, feigning ignorance, say, 'What is happening? Please stop making noise.' Then the perplexed community members will say, 'The sons of so and so are killing each other. What might have occurred? We have always known them as peaceful children.' Then the troublemaker will scornfully say, 'You don't know them? This is how they are always.

Herjok's sons heeded to the good counsel from their wise father and made sure that no outsider, no matter how smart and cunning, could infiltrate their group and turn them against each other. Whenever they had a family issue, they solved it amicably in a brotherly manner, knowing that each and every person under the sun has his own weaknesses, but that these weaknesses did not diminish their value. Even a troublemaker has his own challenges to deal with in life, the first one being that he is a troublemaker himself, causing problems to others. That is why I suggest we in South Sudan also heed to Herjok's time-tested advice.

There are many ways in which the Dinka and the Nuer conflict can destroy South Sudan, but let us consider a few of those ways and their dreadful ramifications.

First, the loss of human lives and property is felt both by the Dinka and the Nuer. In the past, women, children and old people were spared when the two communities were at war, while the animals and other valuables were looted by the wining party. But this has changed since mid-1980s. Today, when the Dinka and the Nuer fight, nothing is spared the wrath of the enemy, whether human beings or material possessions. Even if young women and girls escape the sword, they are taken as prisoners of war, to be married by their captors against their will. As for properties, these are either deliberately destroyed or taken by the attackers as war booty.

From the mid-1980s to the time of writing, many people from both sides have lost their lives and property; others have become disabled, orphaned, widowed, and internally displaced.

Villages and towns have been deserted by people from both sides due to insecurity.

Second, the Dinka and the Nuer conflict damages the image of the two tribes in the eyes of the other communities and before God. God isn't happy when his people go about butchering each other mercilessly in what is fundamentally a war of pride and greed. If the blood of Abel could cry before God in heaven, how do you think God reacts towards the shedding of the innocent blood of the elderly, women, children, lame, blind, mad, drunkards, name it! The image of the Dinka and the Nuer has been sullied in and outside South Sudan to the extent that if one or both names are mentioned, it is often for bad, as they are associated with brutality.

Third, the war between the Dinka and the Nuer also directly or indirectly affects other people inside South Sudan, especially tribes bordering the Dinka and the Nuer, which often contend with the fallout of the conflict of these two communities. At the national level, the animosity between the Dinka and the Nuer sometimes gets disguised as one of the national issues. And whenever a genuine national issue arises, and people try to address it, the hidden Dinka- Nuer animosity will erupt and overshadow such an issue. It is then misconstrued as a Dinka and Nuer issue, pitting Dinka and Nuer against each other and, eventually, the issue fails to receive the national attention that it deserves. When such national issues are treated as tribal issues, they end up compounding the already complex Dinka-Nuer conflict and messing up the actual situation in the process. If serious thinking is not done so as to separate ethnic issues from national issues and give the latter the seriousness they deserve, people's focus will be misguided as national issues get mistaken for Dinka-Nuer issues.

There are two examples to support this argument. When the South Sudanese got discontented and rebelled—Battalion 105 in Bor and Battalion 106 in Ayod in 1983—against the Khartoum government, they didn't do it as Dinka and Nuer but took it as a national issue affecting all the communities of South Sudan and other marginalized people of other parts of Sudan. But during the official formation of the movement, the Sudan People's Liberation Movement (SPLM) and the Sudan People's Liberation Army (SPLA) in 1983, there was a disagreement among the Sudanese that took an ugly turn and became a potential problem between the Dinka and the Nuer. This misdirection of focus ended up causing great loss of lives, destruction of properties, and displacement of people from their ancestral homes, with some ending up as orphans, widows and widowers, maimed and lame, blind, etc. Also, this Dinka-Nuer war almost derailed the movement and made it take longer in achieving its purpose than what should have been the case.

After obtaining their hard-earned independence on 9 July 2011, people thought that the Dinka-Nuer problem had finally been resolved. It was believed that they themselves would feel they had done enough mistakes and not want to repeat them. Alas, what seemed to be normal political wrangling within the ruling party, SPLM—which isn't a Dinka-Nuer entity but a national entity—took a tragic turn and degenerated into a Dinka-Nuer issue on 16 December 2013 in Juba. As this political issue became a Dinka-Nuer problem, it spread like wildfire, setting innocent Dinka and Nuer people against each other and resulting in heavy loss of lives and property from both sides. As I write, there are many refugees in neighbouring countries and others who have sought safety in UN camps and other camps of displaced people inside South Sudan as a result of the hostilities that followed. This is not to mention the many orphans, widows and widowers, those maimed and others who were made blind by this unfortunate war. There are many villages and towns that are deserted and huge chunks of land that lie fallow because there are no people to cultivate it.

It is unfortunate but true to say that the Dinka and the Nuer seem to be experts in misdirecting national issues that belong to all people to themselves and proffering them back to people when they are too hot to handle.

Fourth, the Dinka-Nuer conflict has resulted in the insecurity of the nation. When two elephants fight, the elephants themselves, the grass beneath them and even the small bushes around suffer a lot. Likewise, the war between the Dinka and the Nuer has resulted in insecurity, affecting them as well as other local tribes. At the time of my writing, there is no free movement of people and goods in many places inside South Sudan and also across some national borders. This conflict could also cause insecurity along certain national borders in that the nation's security apparatus could end up being focused on internal security, leaving certain borders unsecured. For instance, South Sudan security forces now pay less attention to the Abyei issue and the border dispute between South Sudan and Sudan due to the current conflict. The Dinka-Nuer war could weaken South Sudan military power, as the two communities contribute the highest number of security personnel in the national army, leaving the nation vulnerable to external attacks.

The only people who may have benefitted from the conflict between the Dinka and the Nuer are the human rights activists, UN Security Council and those concerned with bringing those accused of war crime and human rights violation to justice. These are they who are called in to govern and judge those who are unable to govern and judge themselves worldwide. It is unfortunate that things in South Sudan had to degenerate to this level, necessitating the help of outsiders.

Fifth, the Dinka-Nuer conflict could easily bring about economic collapse in South Sudan. As it has happened before, when the Dinka and the Nuer wage war against each other, the whole nation is thrust into the war mode as well, bringing economic activities to a standstill. As we have seen since the onset of the current conflict in 2013, the movement of goods nationwide has been drastically curtailed. The prices of the few goods in the market have skyrocketed, going beyond the reach of the common people. Many local and foreign investors have been forced to close their businesses. The current inflation, though there is no statement to this effect yet, is very high, and the scarcity of hard currency, especially the US dollar, is making life very hard because it is difficult to import even essential commodities. Oil production and farming have been brought to a standstill. Although people view it as a Dinka-Nuer tribal war, its negative economic effects are national in scope, touching on even none South Sudanese people.

Sixth, the Dinka-Nuer war has a negative effect on national politics. Usually, politics is considered as an art and a science of governance where politicians and other civil servants plan and execute programs to meet national goals and aspirations of their people. The main objective of politics is to design ways and means to alleviate people's suffering or, better still, make their lives comfortable. But the moment the actual voters begin to suffer from political wrangling, they lose faith in politics. The current political dispute that goes back to 2013 has disrupted peace in the nation and made the common man to hate politicking. In fact it will take a long time before real politicians and the government earn the confidence of the people again.

Seventh, the Dinka-Nuer war could, if it persists much longer, result in the disintegration of the nation. The more the Dinka and the Nuer hate and fight each other, the more their staying together as a people of the same nation becomes harder. For them to create a conducive environment to live and work together, they should reconcile their differences and appreciate what unites them while overlooking what divides them. They should also forgive one another for the sake of their peaceful co-existence and national cohesion. But if they try to keep on hating each other, embracing a vengeful attitude, only God knows how they can live as citizens of the same nation without destroying each other and tearing their nation apart in the middle.

Worse still, if the Dinka-Nuer war continues unabated, some of the other tribes in South Sudan that do not like unnecessary conflict may decide to break away from such an unstable nation. In considering this, they may have two options to take. The first option may be to seek ways and means of separating their regions, through violent or non-violent means, from the areas under the control of the Dinka or the Nuer. This means that if they succeed, they will have created their own independent nation(s). The second option may be to align themselves with a strong third party to annex themselves to it.

Eighth, the Dinka-Nuer war could facilitate the plundering of the wealth of South Sudan by outsiders. Whenever members of a family fight among themselves, unkind bystanders get a chance to loot any important assets from the family. It is also common knowledge that when there is anarchy in a market or town, some greedy people take advantage to break in and loot anything they lay their hands on. Looters thrive where confusion abounds, whether it is brought about by fighting families or nations. Hence, if the Dinka and the Nuer keep on dragging the nation to war, they may find themselves leaving their wealth unprotected, thus exposing it to external plunderers.

Chapter Two

How the Dinka and the Nuer
Can Build Up South Sudan

Why Support the Unity of the Dinka and the Nuer

If you love the Dinka and the Nuer, it is better to support what unites them rather than what divides them. If you love the peaceful co-existence of the different communities in South Sudan, it is incumbent on you to work towards what unites them rather than what divides them. Above all, if we want to see a united, prosperous South Sudan, then it is time we sought viable solutions to all our national issues, starting right from the root causes.

Some of the Dinka and Nuer elites who have the unhealthy tendency of fanning the conflict between the two communities need to know that the general wellbeing of the Dinka and the Nuer is far above their narrow interests.

They should not use their innocent people as bait to meet their selfish interests. Instead, such learned individuals ought to work towards the peaceful co-existence of the two communities by supporting what unites them and avoiding what divides them. The Dinka and the Nuer elites plus church and other religious leaders should be the ones to spearhead the urgent reconciliation of their people if they really love them. After all, their happiness is closely linked to their people's happiness and the sadness of the two communities to the sadness of such elites. There is no way a mentally healthy person will rejoice when his people are crying; it is normal to laugh or cry with your people. Hence, it is morally compelling for the Dinka and the Nuer elites to promote the unity of their people for their general welfare as well as for God's glory.

If they don't work for the durable peace between their two communities, they should not expect someone else to do it. This is because they understand their problem better than others do, and they know the best solution for it. The elites should know that the unity of the Dinka and the Nuer is for their own good and the good of the entire South Sudan.

I know of two committees of elders, one comprising Dinka elders and the other Nuer elders. I don't know their specific roles and why they were formed, but I guess that they were intended for working towards the peace of the two communities and, accordingly, for the benefit of the entire nation. To me, the most important task that these two committees should take upon themselves, separately and collectively, before man and God, would be to help the Dinka and the Nuer satisfactorily address their problem, be united and live and work together as brothers and sisters and eventually extend this unity to other communities within South Sudan.

There are a few unhealthy thinkers from other ethnic communities in South Sudan who are in support of the Dinka-Nuer war. One of their devilish proposals is that the Dinka and the Nuer be allowed to kill each other until they become smaller than other tribes. But what such people fail to realize is that the two big communities can't reach the point of killing and reducing their numbers before dragging the smaller communities into the same war of annihilation. A person of sound mind should not encourage two strong guys to fight in a

house full of small children because the little
ones could die of being trampled upon. The
Bible in Hebrews 12:14 urges us to follow
peace with all men. Elsewhere in 1Pet.3:11, the
author tells us to seek peace and pursue it. It is
therefore easy to understand from whence the
spirit that encourages people to kill one another
comes from. The war between the Dinka and
the Nuer translates into a civil war in South
Sudan.

Hence, for the sake of the unity of the Dinka
and the Nuer, and for the sake of the unity of all
the South Sudanese people, it is good for those
who support the Dinka-Nuer war to adjust
their minds to what the Word of God says and
start supporting the unity of the Dinka and the
Nuer instead. They should know that the peace
and happiness of the Dinka and the Nuer is also
their peace and happiness.

Concerning the insensitive foreigners who
support the Dinka-Nuer war, it is very clear
that they neither love the two communities nor
have their welfare or the welfare of the entire
South Sudan at heart. Also, they are clearly
ungodly people. Whatever support, whether
moral or material, that they extend to both
parties is for the destruction of the Dinka and

the Nuer and, by extension, of the South Sudan in general. You should not support people to wage war of destruction and annihilation if you really love them and fear God. If you do so, God and fellow men will judge you harshly. Such people ought to abandon their old divisive policy and begin supporting what unites the Dinka and the Nuer, not what divides them. This way, peace and its benefits will begin to be experienced among the Dinka and the Nuer and, by extension, in South Sudan as a whole. In the end, people will tag them as advocates of peace and development rather than promoters of anarchy and destruction.

Generally, it is unwise when brothers fight, kill one another and destroy their things, only to blame others for encouraging them to fight. You should use your God-given mind to make judgment and determine whether what others are telling you to do is good or bad. If it is good, you should pursue it, but if it is bad, you should reject it. Else, people will keep manipulating you, making you act against your will for their own benefit, and in the end you are the one who will be humiliated.

It is high time the Dinka and the Nuer became masters of their God-given minds and learn to say no when they are being encouraged to fight each other, and to say yes when they are given a message of peace. Blaming your woes on others when you had every opportunity of avoiding trouble is unwise, even if you share the blame for what has befallen you. Moreover, the first people to benefit from the unity of the Dinka and the Nuer are the two communities themselves. Likewise, the first people to suffer from the conflict between the Dinka and the Nuer are they themselves. That is why they should be the first people to support their unity.

The Importance of the Unity between the Dinka and the Nuer

The Americans emphasize the importance of unity among people. That is why they say, "Divided we fall; united we stand". The importance of unity was appreciated even by Solomon of old, who says, "Though one may be overpowered, two can defend themselves. A cord of three strands is not quickly broken" (Eccl.4:12). It is this awareness that has led to the creation of economic and security blocks like NATO (North Atlantic Treaty Organization), EU (European Union), AU (African Union), AL (Arab League), OPEC

(Organization of the Petroleum Exporting Countries), UN (United Nations), UNEP (United Nations Environmental Program), APEC (Asia Pacific Economic Cooperation), ASEAN (Association of Southeast Asian Nations), CARICOM (Caribbean Community Market), CAEU (Council of Arab Economic Unity), EADB (East African Development Bank), ECOWAS (Economic Community of West African States), OAS (Organization of American States), SADCC (Southern African Development Coordination Council), WHO (World Health Organization), etc.

Wanting to teach his sons the importance of unity, one man asked each of his children to come with a little stick. He then tied the sticks together and gave the bundle to each of them in turn to break, but none of them was able to break it. Then he untied the bundle and returned to each boy his stick and asked each boy to break his stick. All of them were able to break their sticks—with very little effort actually. Then the man asked his sons, "Why were you unable to break the bundle and yet effortlessly broke the separate sticks".

"The bundle was hard to break because the

sticks were tied together," they answered, "but the sticks became weak after being divided."

The man used this practical illustration to show his children the importance of unity and concluded by saying, "If you unite like the tied bundle of sticks, you will maintain your strength and overcome any external pressure, but if you do not unite, you will become as vulnerable as the single sticks that were so easy to break."

Following are some of the benefits that will accrue from the unity of the Dinka and the Nuer. First, there will be no unnecessary waste of lives and property among the Dinka and the Nuer, both in the homelands of these two communities and in the rest of South Sudan. Henceforth, South Sudanese children will not be born in war, grow up in war and die in war, not having had the opportunity to realize their potential in life. Peace will enable them to enjoy their God-given resources and the benefits of their labour.

Second, the Dinka and the Nuer will acquire a better image in the eyes of other communities and re-position themselves among the sons and daughters of South Sudan as they unite, work and live together peacefully as people with the common aspiration of building the same nation. They will no longer come across as war-mongers.

Third, the unity of the Dinka and the Nuer will boost the economy of the two tribes as well as that of the entire nation. This is because there will be stability and a peaceful atmosphere that will encourage people to return to their ancestral homes, title their land, and move freely and trade among themselves. Also local and international investors will be able to carry out their businesses for the good of the people.

Fourth, the unity of the Dinka and the Nuer will restore and reshape, both the political landscape of the Dinka and the Nuer and that of the entire nation of South Sudan. The common man in South Sudan will no longer view politics as a national curse but as a means of enabling people realize their individual and collective aspirations. Outsiders will also begin to appreciate the political landscape of South Sudan the moment they feel it is being run in the right way.

Fifth, the unity of the Dinka and the Nuer will tremendously improve the security condition in South Sudan. If the Dinka and the Nuer start to live and work together as brothers and sisters in their homelands and in other parts of South

Sudan, they will also ensure that security in and along national borders is maintained. In fact, some of the able-bodied Dinkas and Nuers will start participating in the maintenance of the national security.

Sixth, the unity of the Dinka and the Nuer will enhance the foreign policy of South Sudan. This is so because if South Sudan starts enjoying security, a stable economy, proper politicking and respect for the rule of law, other nations will desire to strengthen their relationship with the country. They will no longer view South Sudan as a weak but stable nation. Of course strength is admired, but weakness is generally despised.

Seventh, the unity of the Dinka and the Nuer means the protection of their national resources from internal and external vampires. The Dinka and the Nuer, together with the other South Sudanese, will act as a formidable team for protecting the resources within the four corners of the nation.

Eighth, the unity of the Dinka and the Nuer will encourage intermarriage among the South Sudanese. And the more the children are born and brought up in such mixed marriages, the more the chances of sustaining the unity among themselves.

Ninth, the unity of the Dinka and the Nuer will bring God's blessing upon the whole nation of South Sudan. This is because the Prince of Peace bestows his blessings where people live in peace and harmony.

The Unity of the Dinka and the Nuer Leads to National Unity

The unity of the Dinka and the Nuer will engender a socio-economic, cultural and political environment that is favourable for the unity of all South Sudanese people. First of all, this unity will grow and eventually overflow to the neighbouring communities. In other words, the Dinka and the Nuer will start to restore the broken relationships with themselves and with their neighbours. But apart from living in peace between themselves, they need the support of other tribes within the nation. By living peacefully and extending an olive branch to others, other tribes will reciprocate in the same way towards the Dinka and the Nuer. After winning the confidence of their neighbours and establishing durable peace with them, the Dinka and the Nuer and their neighbours will extend the same peaceful co-existence to the rest of tribes in South Sudan. By realizing the tangible dividends of unity among the Dinka and the Nuer and their neighbouring tribes, and for the sake of national unity, these other tribes will likely be drawn to the bigger loop of unity. Like the ripples with a common epicentre, the unity of the Dinka and the Nuer will keep expanding in influence until it affects the entire South Sudan.

There is no single tribe, whether the Dinka or the Nuer, that doesn't value the peace and unity of the South Sudanese people. The main issue is how to bring about such unity, for people just talk and talk about it without doing what is necessary in actualizing it.

Therefore, even after the unity of the Dinka and the Nuer is eventually realized and embraced by all other communities, it will need all of them to maintain and nurture it further for the general welfare of South Sudanese people. National unity is life and prosperity. It is the heart of any nation. But if you handle it carelessly and lose it, you will suffer tremendously before you get it again!

The tragic thing would be for the shortsighted people in and outside South Sudan to ignore or dismiss this urgent call for unity between the Dinka and the Nuer and other communities as insignificant. It would also be very tragic if the few beneficiaries of our national confusion speak louder than peace seekers and convince people to leave the things to continue the way they are now. Let us be heroes in identifying our problems and finding amicable, sustainable solutions. That way, we will thank none other than ourselves, and the Lord of peace will bless us with our young nation abundantly.

Conclusion

The Dinka and the Nuer have a common origin. They are both Nilotes. As a result, they have similar forms of livelihood and share certain cultural practices and values. When it comes to physical features, it is hard to distinguish between a Dinka and a Nuer. The two communities even intermarry. Generally, the two peoples can be broadly categorized as proud, arrogant, courageous, domineering, hot temper, and endowed with the spirit of resilience. In modern life, some of these traits are not worthy to be proud of. The Dinka and the Nuer are the largest tribes in South Sudan, with the Nuer having a marked presence in western Ethiopia.

The beginning of the uneasy relationship between the Dinka and the Nuer can be traced back to the time of British colonization of Sudan, when the colonialists created an unfavourable situation which pitted certain sections of the two communities against one another.

Unfortunately, even after Sudan became independent in 1956, the conflict between the Dinka and the Nuer wasn't fully addressed. Later on, others took advantage of this poor relationship, trying to fan the differences until they resulted in what others term as the war between the Dinka and the Nuer. This conflict reached its peak, both during the second civil war in Sudan between 983-2005 and also the Juba conflict that started in 2013.

The consequences of the Dinka-Nuer war has had a bad affect on the Dinkas and the Nuers and also the entire nation of South Sudan. These include loss of human lives, destruction of individual and collective assets, damage of the image of the Dinka and the Nuer as well as the image of South Sudan as a nation, insecurity, economic breakdown, political instability, poor foreign relationship, disunity among nationals, and unstable government, among other undesirable effects.

It is the high time the Dinka and the Nuer reconciled their differences, forgave one another and forged better, enduring unity between themselves. They should know that they have more to gain in their unity than in their disunity. It is the high time those who engineer the conflict between the two communities stopped and repented of their bad policies and started to support the unity between the Dinka and the Nuer for the good of the two communities and the general welfare of the South Sudanese people. The unity between them will restore their image and the image of South Sudan and bring about economic prosperity, stable security, political maturity, social cohesion, good foreign relationship, and widespread development. There is a lot to gain from unity and a lot to lose from disunity.

If you happen to support the argument advanced in this book, it would pay to act upon it immediately rather than talking and talking about it while things get worse. If you don't support it, let me know what you propose should be done to address these nation-threatening issues, and I will immediately buy into your opinion if I find them helpful to the nation. But if you don't know what to do about it, then keep quiet, and let those who know what to do about it take charge of the situation. However, if your desire is for the current state of affairs to remain and perhaps get worse, may God and others forgive you, and my prayer for you is that you have a quick change of heart.

Unity is strength, but disunity is weakness; unity builds, but disunity destroys. The unity of our people is what matters most in South Sudan. May the Lord make us, South Sudanese, peacemakers and not destroyers of peace!